# An Abridged History of a Landscape

## Ulong and the Eastern Dorrigo Plateau

Wizzenhill Publishing

Copyright © 2020 Rainey Leigh Seraphine, Wizzenhill Publishing

All rights reserved. Without limiting the rights under copyright reserved above, no part of this work/publication may be reproduced, stored in or introduced into a retrieval system, or transmitted, in any form or by any means (electronic, mechanical, print, photocopying, recording or otherwise), without the prior written permission of the copyright owner.

ISBN 978-0-6487768-0-2

Cover photo supplied by

Ulong Ex Servicemen & Women's Club

A heartfelt dedication to

Beth Scaysbrook

and her beautiful words to describe
our beloved Ulong -

'the communal spirit
shines through the landscape'

## Tall Timbers of Dorrigo

The mountain road to Ulong
we've travelled once again
the trees and ferns were glistening
washed clean by recent rain
and O the tall tall timbers
of Eastern Dorrigo
reaching far above us
from gullies way below
and lush the ferns that nestled
with tropic undergrowth
like vines – my heart was clinging
to leave it, I was loathe
in awe, I saw its splendour
as I saw it years ago
when we took the road to Ulong
in the Eastern Dorrigo


poem by
### June M Montgomery

The Coffs Harbour Hinterlands

Photo by Kate Behmer Photography & Design

Decades of ageing have brought me from city to country, where Ulong, the village in the valley has become my resting place. Perched on the Eastern Dorrigo Plateau, cocooned within the smaller hamlets of Timmsvale, Brooklana, Upper and Lower Bobo, I have risen from the coastline up the mountain towards clouds, some 700 metres, and as such I'm a little closer to heaven.

This village has all I need. A small, general store with enchanting café, the Ex-Servicemen & Women's Club and a primary school, dedicated in its yearning to grandly mold the minds of our children, yet more than that, the space to breathe and a serenity where one can really listen.

In her youth, Ulong boasted butchers, baker, blacksmith and hairdresser. The dentist walked to his pain tortured patients and the bush nurse pedalled to wounded and ailing, skilfully manoeuvring her pushbike along horse-and-cart pitted tracks. The weathered, wooden shops, now residences, bear their age with defiant stoicism and I have heard the bakery house still has its slow combustion oven, tired yet intact.

Ulong is drenched in history, but it's European history is short, recorded by the settlers who came here. Her ancient, Aboriginal heritage cries for more. To know her history begs immersion, in a deep primal sense. Their way of life; their innate sense of spirituality and connection to the landscape, their sense of place; none can truly be recorded. Their stories are oral, witnessed only by bare silent footsteps, still whispering through the hills and valleys of the Dorrigo Plateau.

To the east, the village of Lowanna also whispers her history. She too has a general store with post office and enchanting cafe and both are the thriving pulse for all who live here.

photo supplied by Ulong Ex Servicemen & Women's Club

How magnificently serene it is to sit here with friends and family, sharing delights from Splinters on Pinc, the restaurant within the Club. The chill of winter does not deter as souls, flesh and bone warm to the brazen flames of the outside fire pit. Our children and grandchildren, impervious to weather and secure in community, play while platypus dive down their watery depths as ducks, white cockatoos and all manner of other bird life flock to the lake.

How splendid it is to come out of winter hibernation, our souls ready to infuse with the buds of Spring and rejoice with nine hours of live music, frivolity, food and dance during the Club's Magic Mountain Music Festival, provided free for the community. Our club is also a life sharing pulse.

It is now time to start our brief, historic trek around Ulong and imagine life, long before European settlement.

## Indigenous Heritage

The Gambalamam clan of the Gumbaynggirr nation, traditionally a coastal tribe of the Coffs Harbour region, travelled west to the Dorrigo Plateau during warmer months and named the area Dundurrigo, translated as stringybark, one of the tree species prevalent.[1] Archaeology shows their existence some 5000 years prior to colonisation. Early Europeans named the area Don Dorrigo, apparently after a Spanish general, so there is dispute with the etymology of the name. Irrespective, it is officially recorded by the Geographical Names Register of NSW as derived from Indigenous language.[2]

The Gumbaynggirr used fire for land management, burning access tracks up through the rainforest, naturally diversifying flora and fauna growth. As such, different species flourished. Unlike their coastal landscape, the rainforest provided a rich source of fruits and medicines, materials for fishing and making hunting nets, water containers and dilly bags. During these visits, sacred places were maintained for ceremonies and rituals invoking good health for all and Country. Ceremonies also taught their law.[3]

Bora ring on Dorrigo Plateau

Bora rings were created and used for Aboriginal ceremonies - picture retrieved from the National Parks of NSW, Fact Sheet 14, Human impacts on the Dorrigo Plateau

---

1   National Parks of NSW, Factsheet 14, NPWS 2015/0277, Human impacts on the Dorrigo plateau, p. 1, cited at nationalparks.nsw.gov.au

2   Dorrigo Chamber of Commerce, History of the Dorrigo Area, cited 16 May 2018 at http://dorrigo.com:80/community/the-history-of-dorrigo/135-history-of-the-dorrigo-area.html

3   National Parks of NSW, Factsheet 14, NPWS 2015/0277, Human impacts on the Dorrigo plateau, p. 2, cited at nationalparks.nsw.gov.au

In 1832, after thousands of years of sole habitation, the Gambalamam met their first white European, Richard Craig. Upon escaping the penal settlement at Moreton Bay, he found his way to Dorrigo Plateau. It is hard to fathom the Gambalamam's perceptions at seeing this white man, but I feel it was with a sense of innocent curiosity as he was welcomed by the Gumbaynggirr people. They allowed him to join their hunting trips and learn their landscape. He is recorded as the first contact between European and Aboriginal in this area.[4] The Dorrigo Chamber of Commerce in their History of Dorrigo, confirm Craig was known for his seasonal travels and companionable relationship with the Indigenous. Craig is also the first European to have full knowledge of the landscape of the Dorrigo Plateau.[5] I particularly like this peace filled snippet of Dorrigo's history.

I did not site evidence of major conflict between the colonists and Indigenous on Dorrigo Plateau, although I didn't thoroughly search for it. Would it be in ignorance to assume there was none? I have lived in areas where a bloody history resides and the aura was different, almost palpable. Suffice it to say, that aura is not here in our valleys and hills.

Ulong also has indigenous evidence. In 1920, a stone axe was found by one of the first settlers, Thomas Timms. The axe lay close to a Crab Apple tree which stood roughly 150 feet high. Close inspection showed its trunk engraved with stepping pockets and it is believed these steps were carved by Aboriginals so they could scale the trunk and retrieve honey from the bee hives wedged high in the canopy. These hives were a common sight and the honey is described by settlers as lush, wild tasting and palatable. The Indigenous skill and tenacity with climbing the trees, risking angry, swarming bees was recognised by the early white settlers of the plateau. The stone axe and other artefacts were later sent to England.[6]

---

4   National Parks of NSW, Factsheet 14, NPWS 2015/0277, Human impacts on the Dorrigo plateau, p. 2, cited at nationalparks.nsw.gov.au

5   Dorrigo Chamber of Commerce, History of the Dorrigo Area, cited 16 May 2018 at http://dorrigo.com:80/community/the-history-of-dorrigo/135-history-of-the-dorrigo-area.html

6   Jess Bell, 1977, A Pioneer and the Eastern Dorrigo, Central North Coast Newspaper Company Pty Ltd, Coffs Harbour, National Library of Australia ISBN 0909228043 p. 19

# Early Landscape use of the Dorrigo Plateau

It is impossible to bifurcate Eastern Dorrigo from Dorrigo itself and the effects of humanisation on her landscape. This plateau was formed by eruption of the Ebor volcano some 20 million years ago. Basalt from the volcano covered ancient granite and formed the Dorrigo escarpment, part of the Great Escarpment of eastern Australia, also nestled within the Great Dividing Range.[7]

The plateau spans two hundred and fifty square miles and is watered by the Little Nymboida River, the Bobo River, Wild Cattle Creek, Bielsdown Creek and the Little Murray River, all permanent water courses and tributaries of the Clarence River.

Although the plateau was not officially settled, by the 1840s, cedar getters were travelling the Bellinger River northward in search of precious timber, but their tenacious efforts were confounded by an escarpment below the plateau. Around seventeen years later, pit sawyers defied the mountain terrain and setting up camps, felled their bounty, sailing logs along the Eastern Dorrigo rivers rushing down from mountain to sea, to be made ready for shipment.[8] Fifty years later, all Red Cedar on the plateau was logged and so began the harvesting of other valued timbers.[9] But timber wasn't the only precious resource in the area.

European colonisers discovered a rich source of valuable ores. Gold fever raged and miners set up camps, from the Orara Gold Fields through to the Eastern Dorrigo Plateau.[10] We drive past the entrance to one such goldmine on the mountain road and it fills my imagination with times long ago.

---

[7] C. Ollier, Geomorphology and tectonics of the Dorrigo Plateau, Journal of Geological Society of Australia, Vol 29, 1982, Issue 3-4, Pages 431-435.

[8] Orara Valley Historical Society, no date, Rising from the Ashes, The Ulong Ex Serviceman's, The Eastern Dorrigo Pioneering Spirit, ISBN 0-9751722-0-4 National Library of Australia.

[9] National Parks of NSW, Factsheet 14, NPWS 2015/0277, Human impacts on the Dorrigo plateau, p. 2, cited at nationalparks.nsw.gov.au

[10] Ibid, p. 21

Photo by Rainey Goulet

The old gold mine, in Bushman's Range Road off the Eastern Dorrigo Way.
Long closed to the public, it is still a rich source of historic value.

Photo by Rainey Goulet

Such a wonderful map at the entrance to George's Goldmine and as I look intently, I become a pirate 'argh', a land pirate that is, 'tis not for me to sail high seas!

The upper reaches of the Little Nymboida River carry gold and other parts of the Bobo and Wild Cattle Creek are metalliferous. These areas also abound with wild bush turkeys, a valuable source of food for fevered, poverty-stricken miners and it is said that turkeys around the Little Nymboida river were found to have specks of gold in their gizzards.[11]

Bobo River                                                                 Photo by Rachel Cole

---

11   Ibid, p. 23

## European Settlement on the Plateau

Settlement of the Dorrigo Plateau commenced 118 years after the First Fleet arrived in New South Wales and many Europeans; gold prospectors and timber getters alike, walked from their camps on the plateau down to the Bellingen Court House in their bid to win allotment rights to the lush land above.[12] The date was 17 September 1906.

Bellingen Court House, 17 September 1906, men awaiting the land ballot results.
Picture from Orara Historical Society

The ballot offered 129 blocks, ranging from 134 to 457 acres and a further ten blocks were opened in 1912. Land was valued between $2.50 and $4.50 an acre (current equivalent) and blocks were offered under Conditional Purchase Lease, requiring successful applicants to show one hundred pounds worth of improvement to their land each year, plus part payment of the unimproved value of the land and a minimum

---

12  Ibid, p. 19

residency of at least three years. Failure to meet these conditions would revert the land to the Crown.[13]

Land improvement was arduous with nothing but axe and fire. Once dense scrub lay ripped from the soil, the wait for transition to tinder-dry conditions was long and not until burnt, would exposed ground be ready for fodder and fruit tree planting. It was a time-consuming process providing little sustenance for spouse and children before the first milking and sale of cream.

## A Road and Settlers Herald a Change in Landscape

Early settlement had challenges. The mountain road was a track, suitable only for single file horse and rider. Gradually, settlers widened and secured the road using a process known as corduroy. Due to heavy rainfall, virgin dirt was often boggy causing mayhem during the winding steep climb as horse drawn carts were burdened with furniture and supplies. Corduroy was a process of cutting timber slabs, or using poles to lay across the mud, infilling with dirt to secure the wood. This process was used in the boggiest of areas where the forest canopy prevented sunshine from drying the ground. Evidence of this practice can still be seen on some sections of the Eastern Dorrigo Way.[14]

Picture of Eastern Dorrigo Way, 1929, from: A Pioneer and the Eastern Dorrigo[15]

---

13  Ibid, p. 20

14  Jess Bell, 1977, A Pioneer and the Eastern Dorrigo, Central North Coast Newspaper Company Pty Ltd, Coffs Harbour, National Library of Australia ISBN 0909228043 p. 9

15  Ibid, p. 33

Maintaining, let alone tarring rural roads was hardly considered a priority by local government, and I know we could all agree, little has changed. Complaints in the Don Dorrigo newspaper were rife before council finally hired a permanent maintenance worker in 1950. Tarring later began but was a slow process, one kilometre at a time over many years.

A local story in the 1980s claims it took a visit on the plateau from Prime Minister, Bob Hawke, to add some heavy weight to inspire roadwork completion by local government. He was visiting his friend, actor Jack Thompson who owns land in Ulong. Apparently, Bob didn't like the winding dirt road and joined the complainants in their frustrated demands to council.[16]

But it wasn't until the mid-1990s that the road to Ulong was completed. From there, the virgin rutted road to Dorrigo still challenges an unwary driver, who finds relief at the hamlets of Megan and Cascade, proudly boasting their few metres of tar.

So the dry season dust still floats to greet the forest canopy and the wet season bog still challenges those driving the steep mountain inclines. Locals, of course, are long used to it and travel the road regularly, but not I! A pioneering trip for me, from Ulong to Dorrigo saw my van fill with a dust storm of massive proportions. I could barely see my dog, perched on her seat in the back. Who knew the seals on the back door were long withered? I swear I can still feel the dust up my nose when I think on it!

---

[16] Orara Valley Historical Society, no date, Rising from the Ashes, The Ulong Ex Serviceman's, The Eastern Dorrigo Pioneering Spirit, ISBN 0-9751722-0-4 National Library of Australia, p. 114

*A Tourist blog writes:*
*The road from Ulong to Dorrigo is some of the worst unsealed road I have ever taken a road bike on, and it's a good 25 k long. It took me ages to cover this road despite being a very capable dirt road rider. In places the road reduced to a 4-wheel drive track with large sections of the soil washed away leaving only rocky outcrops exposed. You need to approach rock with plenty of care when equipped with road tyres. Finally, I made it across and on the approach to Dorrigo the road is again excellent and soon I was at Dangar falls, one of the dozen or more excellent waterfalls that are scattered about this area.*
*https://www.motorcycleparadise.net/2010/01/tour-meltdown.html*

Although Red Cedar was long gone, Eastern Dorrigo held huge pockets of hard and softwood timbers, such as Coachwood, Tallowood, Silky Oak, Jade Basswood, Mountain Cedar and Rose Mahogany, with Hoop Pine one of the most prolific and valuable. Many settlers, desperate to feed their families as quickly as possible, saw value in timber milling with its short term financial gain compared to long term scrub clearing and farming before income was produced.

In 1898, Paul Mulhearn, originally from Richmond River, arrived on the plateau with gold fever; but discovered his gaze was drawn to tall trees above, not the gold speckled creek beds at his feet. He returned to Richmond River and worked until he could afford a bullock team. Around ten years later with bullocks in tow, he commenced cutting pine logs, keeping them stored with their bark intact, ready for transportation to Coffs Harbour. But it was a frustrating wait for the road to be made from Coramba as his logs lay useless, void of income. He realised the need for producing milled timber on the spot, saving time, costs and difficulty of transporting massive logs and I cannot refute his logic.[17]

By 1925, Mulhearn and other settlers had built sawmills at Ashton, Ulong, Upper Bobo, Lowanna, Morora, Brooklana and Timmsvale, providing employment for incoming settlers and their families. One prospective mill owner ordered a steam engine to power his mill. But with no delivery service to the plateau, he had to drive the engine from Coffs Harbour, through Coramba and up the mountain, stopping every three miles to fell timber to keep the boiler going. Without room to store enough wood for such a long drive, it took many gruelling days to reach the plateau.[18] The stamina of early settlers should not be understated and I wonder if we, their descendants could achieve the same.

Felling timber was hard, dangerous work and early settlement meant many men worked alone in dense scrub. One such man, a young logger, is testament to the danger. The weight of timber he'd cut and loaded broke the spindle bar attached to his bullock team and a twenty-metre log rolled off, pinning his leg against a rocky outcrop. The weighty log was impossible to move for a man on his own but survival is a strong instinct. He severed the trapped leg with his knife and burned the bloodied stump to stop infection. Fortitude is a word that comes to mind but even then, it doesn't seem enough to describe the horror I feel when picturing this scene! He then climbed onto his lead bullock and rode back to camp for help. Later making himself a wooden leg, it became useful as a wedge when splitting and debarking trees. Far from bemoaning his lost limb (as most would), he found the wooden leg a great asset. It gave protection against snake bite and the occasional slip of the broad axe blade, although he admitted termites

---

17 Beth Scaysbrook, A Patchwork of People who helped create the fabric of the Eastern Dorrigo Community in the 1900s, Kempsey NSW, 2003

18 Jess Bell, 1977, A Pioneer and the Eastern Dorrigo, Central North Coast Newspaper Company Pty Ltd, Coffs Harbour, National Library of Australia ISBN 0909228043, p. 34

were a worry.[19] One of the creeks is unofficially named after him, One Legged Logger Creek and I think it's a great, though small tribute to this intrepid young man.

Small section of a massive log   Photo from Orara Valley Historical Society

Communication was also a challenge for mill owners on the plateau, so the Mulhearn Bros Pigeon Post provided a perfect solution. With large distances between each mill, relaying vital news was the responsibility of trained pigeons and they were unrivalled in their expertise. One bird managed to transport messages some sixty miles in less than an hour; a trip that would have taken a car over three hours on the winding hilly roads.[20]

In 1921, a Hydro Electric Plant was opened in Dorrigo and an enterprising Timmsvale timber miller was convinced a hydro mill would suit his property as it bordered permanent waters of the Little Nymboida River. Laborious work of dam construction did

---

19  Orara Valley Historical Society, no date, Rising from the Ashes, The Ulong Ex Serviceman's, The Eastern Dorrigo Pioneering Spirit, ISBN 0-9751722-0-4 National Library of Australia, p. 51
20  Orara Valley Historical Society, no date, Rising from the Ashes, The Ulong Ex Serviceman's, The Eastern Dorrigo Pioneering Spirit, ISBN 0-9751722-0-4 National Library of Australia, p. 37

not deter, and intense planning, engineering and erection of the structure ploughed on until his goal was achieved.

The first hydro mill triumphantly commenced its operations around 1925 but a new challenge was discovered in the process. On rare occasions, the turbine would suddenly stop and inspection would show a massive eel shredded throughout the machinery, a truly bloody mess.[21] Yet dauntless in the face of such challenges, the mill went on to provide quality hardwood and softwood, highly praised in Sydney. It's interesting to note the coachwood was favoured for making boot heels.[22]

Picture by Katie Sibio Ulong General Store

---

21  Ibid, p. 15

22  Jess Bell, 1977, A Pioneer and the Eastern Dorrigo, Central North Coast Newspaper Company Pty Ltd, Coffs Harbour, National Library of Australia ISBN 0909228043 p. 15

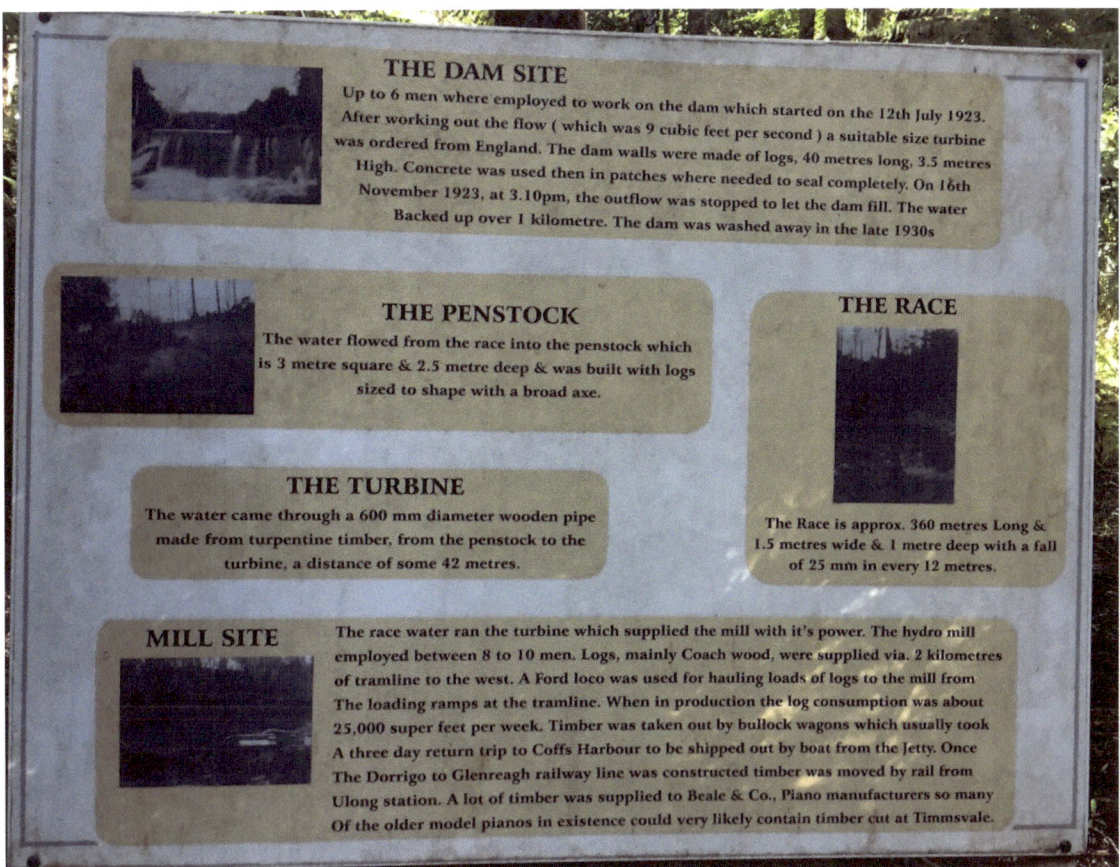

Photo by Katie Sibio Ulong General Store

During the second world war, timber milling was a protected industry and the mills on the Eastern Dorrigo Plateau were greatly valued. Many sons of the first World War veterans enlisted, but those who stayed to work the mills came under the control of the government. Holidays were reduced to four days per year and inspectors regularly visited to supervise the smooth and efficient running of timber production. Much of the timber sent to allied forces in England and Darwin was used for making rifle butts, army tent poles, truck bodies and anything else needed for warfare.[23]

Between Ulong and Lowanna, an area known as Ashton's Flat was used as an army training camp. Dense scrub was considered good training ground for an estimated one thousand troops, to practice jungle warfare tactics before heading overseas for battle.[24]

---

23  Ibid, p. 20

24  Ibid, p. 21

# The North Coast Railway Line Opens, Glenreagh to Dorrigo

Bobo Railway Bridge                                         Photo from Orara Historical Society

In 1924, the Glenreagh to Dorrigo line was officially opened, after fourteen years of erratic construction due to difficult terrain and financial constraints.

Around 700 men lay tracks for the railway line with sixteen of them working on tunnels, carved through the mountain. These tunnels took two years to build, using early forms of jackhammers and conditions were primitive and dangerous.[25] Geological formation of the area from Glenreagh to Dorrigo caused many rock slides onto the line which almost aborted the project, but as the worst areas were close to completion, work pushed on.[26]

---

25  Orara Valley Historical Society, no date, Rising from the Ashes, The Ulong Ex Serviceman's, The Eastern Dorrigo Pioneering Spirit, ISBN 0-9751722-0-4 National Library of Australia, p. 127

26  Ibid, p. 127

Due to steep terrain up the mountain and drenching rainfall, many landslides occurred causing the track to slip, despite heavy gauged steel used on the steepest inclines. Derailment of carriages with the weight of timber was not uncommon.

Photo from Orara Historical Society

The rail line was a turning point for establishment of the Eastern Dorrigo Plateau, not only for excited passengers and their new ease of travel, but also for the vast amounts of timber that were transported to Coffs Harbour and further afield.[27]

---

27   Ibid, p. 122

Stations were built from Glenreagh to Timber Top, Moleton, Lowanna, Ulong, Brooklana, Cascade, Lloyds Siding, Briggsvale, Megan, Leigh and Dorrigo. Many mills were built alongside railway stations and sidings for ease of transport.

The cutest little railway station I have ever seen - Ulong Siding, Photo supplied by Ulong Ex Servicemen's Club

Steam trains were replaced by diesel locomotives after 1958 but with the constant landslides and reconstructions necessary, in 1972 the railway closed; costs were outweighing profit! Dark rusty rail tracks are mostly covered by grass and scrub now, but history cries for remembrance and a group of dedicated historians started the Glenreagh Mountain Railway, a non-profit organisation with the aim of operating a heritage railway line from Glenreagh to Ulong for tourists and locals alike.

To date, its completion has not been successful but their determined efforts continue regardless. How brilliant it would be to experience such majestic rides up and through landscape of forest and granite as clouds of steam drift through the canopy and dark tunnels, although I suspect the sleeping bats in the tunnels would not agree!

Photo supplied by Ulong Ex-Servicemen & Women's Club

Signage at Pine Ave, entrance to the Village
in the Valley

## Conclusion

Since volcanic eruption some 20 million years ago, natural evolution of rainforest and plateau, silent footprints of the Gumbaynggirr and axe then machination of white settlers all show their mark on the Dorrigo landscape. Yet it is visual beauty and I cannot say if any beauty has been lost with humanisation, for I was not witness to the process. If any was, it must have been an other-worldly kind of beauty. Of course, coastlines and some may even say, 'cityscapes' are resplendent in all their glory, but Ulong's peaceful landscape has soul.

Little has changed since early white settlement of Eastern Dorrigo. Descendants still reside and speak their stories of ancestry long past. Untouched by modern urbanisation; like those before us, our thirst is quenched by tanks holding life-giving waters of pure rain and sparkling winding creeks and rivers.

I concur with author and historian, Deborah Bird Rose. A sense of Place does not require a sequence of time, in the lineal sense, to gain an understanding of landscape and her history. All is found on the ground at our feet. All is present in the land and her memory and all is alive in our experience of now; past and present become indivisible.[28] Ancient stories, both Indigenous and white, whisper on the ripples of her creeks and rivers; they rustle through the leaves of her forest timbers and they ride on the wind through her lush valleys. It is a sentient landscape of shared Place.

The mills are now silent but for the echo of ghosts and the gnawing of termites. The metal of her rail track; abandoned and rusted lays still, shrouded by flora in its strive for life eternal. And I sit on my verandah and listen to those ancient whispers, a little closer to heaven.

---

28  Deborah Bird Rose "Writing Place" in *Writing histories: imagination and narration* eds. Ann McGrath and Ann Curthoys (Clayton: Monash University ePress 2009), p. 51

My verandah with canine hiding behind the birdbath.

www.ingramcontent.com/pod-product-compliance
Lightning Source LLC
Chambersburg PA
CBHW041429010526
44107CB00045B/1546